C000104531

TOPLESS

TOPLESS

Miles Tredinnick

ALSO BY MILES TREDINNICK
Laugh? I Nearly Went To Miami!
It's Now Or Never!
Fripp

More details at

www.milestredinnick.com

To Robert Goodman
whose encouragement never faltered.
Many thanks.

Copyright © 2006 Miles Tredinnick

The moral right of the author has been asserted.

Apart from any fair dealing for the purposes of research or private study,
or criticism or review, as permitted under the Copyright, Designs and Patents
Act 1988, this publication may only be reproduced, stored or transmitted, in
any form or by any means, with the prior permission in writing of the
publishers, or in the case of reprographic reproduction in accordance with
the terms of licences issued by the Copyright Licensing Agency. Enquiries
concerning reproduction outside those terms should be sent to the publishers.

First published in 2000 by
Comedy Hall Books

Matador
9 De Montfort Mews
Leicester LE1 7FW, UK
Tel: (+44) 116 255 9311 / 9312
Email: books@troubador.co.uk
Web: www.troubador.co.uk/matador

ISBN 1 905237 75 8

Typeset in 11pt Stempel Garamond by Troubador Publishing Ltd, Leicester, UK

Matador is an imprint of Troubador Publishing Ltd

All rights whatsoever in this play are strictly reserved, and application for professional or amateur performance should be made before rehearsal to: Miles Tredinnick, c/o Troubador Publishing Ltd, 9 De Montfort Mews, Leicester LE1 7FW.

NO PERFORMANCE MAY BE GIVEN WITHOUT A LICENCE.

TOPLESS

First presented in London by Open Top Productions
in association with The Big Bus Company on
September 14th 1999, with the following cast.

Sandie …...……………………………..….. Rachael Carter

Directed by Martin Bailey

*The open-top deck of a London sightseeing bus on a
summer's day.*

TOPLESS

The front end of an open-top London sightseeing bus showing the windscreen, the two front rows of seats and the top of the stairwell. There is a bus bell button on the top of the stairwell rail. NB: It is up to the Director how the play is staged. If you want to use back-projection photos/videos/film of the sights, use them. If you want Sandie's words to paint the pictures unaided, don't. It is entirely up to your imagination.

When the lights come up, SANDIE is coming up the stairs, carrying a holdall bag, which she puts down on the floor. She takes her microphone out of it and plugs it in. She then addresses her tourists, (the audience). SANDIE is a Londoner in her mid-30s. She's neatly dressed in blazer and skirt and very bubbly. She wears a photo ID card pinned to her lapel. She's very likeable and has an infectious giggle.

She reads from a clipboard in dreadful cod-French.

SANDIE:

Bienvenue a Londres et Bienvenue chez "London Topless Buses". Le "Topless" est le moyen ideal de visiter sans effort les sites touristques de Londres. Je m'appelle Sandie et notre chauffeur est Sid… *(She realises something is wrong and shouts down the stairwell.)* Sid? Are you sure this is the group from Calais? Because they don't seem particularly French to me. They've what? Cancelled? Oh. Well thanks for telling me. *(Facing audience.)* So you all speak English do you? Well I won't be needing that. *(She puts the clipboard down on one of the front seats.)* Hi everyone and welcome to London.

My name's Sandie and I'm your tour guide. How are you all? Everyone OK? I'm feeling absolutely brilliant today. I am. Honestly. Now I know what you're thinking. The wheel's turning but the hamster's dead. But don't worry, I haven't got going yet. I'm building up to my tour de force and believe me it'll be worth waiting for. We're going to have a fabulous tour. Now 'cos I thought you were all going to be foreign I've brought along a few *visual aids* to jazz things up a bit. *(She opens her bag and throws out various soft toy London souvenirs into the audience starting with a miniature Big Ben.)* This is Big Ben which we'll be seeing later. Who wants Big Ben? *(She then takes out a little Beefeater doll.)* And here's one of the Yeoman Warders you'll see down the Tower. *(Next she produces a policeman's helmet and throws it to a man.)* Evening all! *(She salutes him and bends her legs.)* Love your helmet sir. Smashing. *(She holds up a large plastic cigar.)* And what's this one? It's Winston Churchill ain't it. *(She throws it to someone.)* You hold that and wave it when I get to me Churchill bit. *(She then holds up something wrapped in silver foil.)* And what have we got 'ere? Oh me sandwiches. Only cheese and tomato I'm afraid. If anyone wants to do a swop later I'm game. Provided it's not meat. I'm a veggie. Right, that's the basics dealt with so off we go. *(She presses the bus bell button twice. We hear the ding-ding.)* Now our driver is called Sid, he's the best driver in the country. Hopeless in town but in the country he's brilliant!

The bus starts up. It jerks off. SANDIE grabs a safety rail to steady herself. From now to the end

of the play street noises can be heard where
appropriate.

See what I mean!! Hold on tight! Right, now I'm
going to take you on a fabulous trip around
London. I'm going to show you all the big sights.
Trafalgar Square, Big Ben, The London Eye, St
Paul's Cathedral, all the way down to the Tower
of London. So sit back and enjoy yourselves. If
you've got any questions keep them to yourselves!
I haven't got time for questions; I'll be too busy
talking! I'm the original motormouth, me.

Now we're kicking off in Piccadilly Circus...
(Brightly coloured lights in background.)

Where are all the elephants I hear you asking?
And the clowns? Where are the clowns? Well
there aren't any. The word 'circus' is a Latin
word. It means roundabout or circle. Behind the
electric signs is Soho. Oh yes? I see a few of you
men smiling at the mere mention of the name. It's
a night place ladies. You know, clubs and stuff. I
used to be a stripper once you know. I did. I'm
not ashamed of it. I used to work in this dump

called *Madame Bridget's Hot Bodies A Go-Go Club*. I was a topless table dancer. I was. I only did it for the money. I was a bit desperate I have to admit. I'd been on the dole for twelve months and then I saw this ad in the paper for dancers and went along. Had to jack it in though. I used to get giddy standing on the tabletops in me high heels, to say nothing of the sparks I got off the pole! So I left and the next job I got was this. So I'm still topless but this way I'm out in the open air. T'riffic!

Over on your right there is the statue Londoners call Eros, *the Greek God of lurve*. They say that if you stand underneath it on the stroke of midnight and declare your love to your beloved, that love will last a lifetime. Aaaahhhh. I'm not sure that's true. I met my husband Duncan under there one night and my goodness have we had our share of problems. Still you don't want to hear about my troubles with Duncan do you? Of course you don't, you're all here to see the sights.

On the left is Shaftesbury Avenue, that's where all the theatres are. Actually the first time I met

Duncan wasn't under Eros, it was on this bus. Not that he was actually *on* the bus, he sort of ran *into* it. On his motorbike. Made a big dent at the front. It was over there on the corner of Regent Street wasn't it Sid? My goodness, what a carry-on that was. Duncan claimed it was Sid's fault but we won't go into that. Anyway I got talking to Duncan and I found I really liked him. He was gorgeous. *The spitting image of Mel Gibson.* He had long hair and the most beautiful green eyes. And he was all leathered up. I like a man in leather. Of course he didn't sound like Mel Gibson 'cos he came from Manchester. Spoke *like that.* You know like the *Oasis* boys. And of course he was half Chinese on his mother's side. So if you can imagine a leathered up, half Chinese long haired Mel Gibson look-alike who sounded *like that*, well that was Duncan. He was gorgeous. Anyway he... Oh, straight ahead of you is Leicester Square. That's where all the movie premieres are held. Do you know what Duncan told me he did when I first met him? He said he worked in films so I thought hello, hello bit of glamour here, know what I mean girls? Turned out not to be films as in movies as in Hollywood but films as in snapshots as in Cricklewood. He works in one of those places where you drop your holiday pics in and come back an hour later and discover what a crap photographer you are. It's called *Well Developed*.

Cut brightly coloured lights.

We're now in the Haymarket. Back in the seventeenth century this is where you brought your horses and gave them hay and stables and things whenever you came to London. Anyway, where was I? Oh yes. Duncan, he asked me out. We tried to blag our way into *Stringfellow's* by telling the bouncer Duncan was Mel Gibson. Didn't work though. Turned out the bouncer hated Mel Gibson. Thought he looked like a girl. Honestly! Some people...

Ah, now on your left is Orange Street. That's where the street walkers used to ply their trade back in the old days. It was a whores' paradise. They'd do anything for a shiny sixpence. Up with the crinoline down with the knickers...

AS VICTORIAN WHORE: (East End accent.)
Wot's your fancy sir? Oooh! That'll cost you an
extra shiny sixpence if you want me to do *that*.

It was a huge red light district. If you want a laugh
look at that road sign. (*She points.*) "*Humps for
100 yards*".

On your right is the musical *The Phantom of the
Opera*. I haven't actually seen it myself. It's
always sold out. I've heard it's quite good. All
about this beautiful girl with a great aria who falls
in love with some weird looking musical genius.
Andrew Lloyd Webber. He wrote it didn't he? He
writes all the shows.

On the right is a street called Pall Mall. Named
after King Charles II's balls. He used to get people
to whack 'em. With mallets. All the knobs would
stand in a line and whack away. It was a sort of
Italian game a bit like croquet. Very popular I
believe. Pall Mall was one of the first streets to be
lit with gas lamps. Probably so they could have a
few night matches.

Anyway to cut a long story short I saw Duncan off and on for about three weeks. Trouble was when I was off he was on. Some slag called Carol. She worked at the Virgin megastore in Oxford Street and got him half-price CDs. I only found out about her by accident. Whenever I went round his, there were CD boxes all over the place. I knew he was up to something. For one thing he didn't have a CD player. And for another I found her soaking in the bathtub. Bitch. So we had a big row as you'd imagine and I told him it was over but he called me later and said he was sorry and would I at least meet him for a drink. So like a fool I agreed. We arranged to meet under Eros, *the Greek God of lurve,* and of course he said he was sorry and I said I'd forgive him and we kissed and hugged and it was all lovey-dovey. Flippin' hell, if I knew then what I know now I would've pushed him into the bleedin' traffic!

National Gallery on the left, loads of paintings. We're now in Trafalgar Square. Laid out to commemorate the Battle of Trafalgar in 1805. That was a naval battle between the British and the combined forces of France and Spain. Won by us under that man on top of his column, Horatio, Lord Nelson. Admiral of the Fleet.

On the other side is the South African High Commission, South Africa House. See the golden springbok leaping out on the corner of the building? Doesn't it look beautiful? Up there on the balcony was where President Nelson Mandela waved to thousands of people in the square a few years ago. Did you see it on TV? It was brill. I was here. And on that day, and that day only, we had two Nelsons in Trafalgar Square. Not as many pigeons as there used to be. In the old days it was the only place in London where you could feed the birds and have a pigeon sit on your head. And that's sit. Spelt S.I.T.

Fade-up the sound of horses' hooves clip-clopping along Whitehall.

Oh look, quick! There's the Household Cavalry on their way to Horse Guards' Parade. Don't they look handsome? The Queen's Life Guard. They're not supposed to talk to you. In fact if you ask them a question you won't get an answer. Some ladies tuck their phone numbers into the men's boots hoping to get a phone call later when they're off duty. I did that once when I was about seventeen. I wrote something like 'Hi. My name's Sandie and I'd love to go out with you' followed by my phone-number. Nothing happened for five weeks and then I got a call from some old cobbler who was re-heeling the boot. He was very disappointed. He thought Sandie was the name of one of the Horse Guards.

Fade-out the horses' hooves.

Can you see those big black gates ahead of you on the right? They guard the most famous address in this country. Number 10 Downing Street. That's where the Prime Minister works. I'm not really into politics. Just a load of men in suits having affairs with their secretaries. (*This strikes some sort of chord. She pauses.*) Duncan looks good in a suit. When he bothers to wear one. If we're going out somewhere special. Like a wedding. I love a wedding don't you? Everybody dressed up with somewhere to go. It was at a wedding that Duncan proposed to me. It was my brother Tim who was getting hitched. He's in corporate catering and he fell in love with Nikki who butters the sandwiches. (Nikki spells her name with 2Ks by the way; she's a bit particular. Tends to look down on other Nikki's that spell theirs with one K or the more traditional CK). Anyway, it was a great day. Duncan was Best Man. He had to make a speech of course. God it was funny. He stood up and clinked a fork against a glass to get some quiet and guess what? The glass smashed. Bits went flying everywhere. Some of it landed in the bride's grandfather's ice-cream sundae. He didn't notice though. Just carried on eating. He thought it was bits from the nut brittle topping. It was only when his tongue started bleeding that he knew something was up. Laugh? We never stopped. You had to be there really...

Fade up the sound of Big Ben chiming four o'clock.

We're now coming into Parliament Square, the political centre of London. Who's got Big Ben?

Hold it up then, wave it round. There's the real thing on your left. Big Ben's not the name of the clock; it's the name of the enormous bell inside the tower. Weighs thirteen and a half tons. Named after Sir Benjamin Hall. Good job his name wasn't Sir Richard Hall. Eh?

Right who's got the Churchill cigar? The Houses of Parliament is where Winston Churchill had that famous run in with Bessie Braddock. Has anyone heard that one? (*She uses a plastic cigar to impersonate Churchill.*) What happened was Winston Churchill came back from lunch one afternoon slightly, you know, intoxicated. Sounds discourteous to say he was pissed so let's just say he was merry, all right? In fact he was as merry as a newt. Probably had one too many of the old brandies down his club. Anyway he bumps into this Bessie Braddock who can't stand the sight of him. She smells his breath and in a very loud voice so everyone can hear she shouts out "Winston Churchill. You are drunk. DRUNK!" And he turns around looks her right in the eye and says "Mrs Braddock. You are ugly. UGLY! But in the morning I shall be sober." Oh he was one with the one-liners that Churchill. If he'd been around today he probably wouldn't have gone into politics. More than likely he'd have been writing gags for some TV sitcom. He would. He could knock 'em out. I'll give you another example of his quick-fire-wit. It happened between Churchill and Lady Nancy Astor. She was an American from Virginia and the first female Member of Parliament to take her seat in the House. Anyway, one afternoon all the MPs were in there, you know, debating and what-have-you, when Lady Astor lost her rag at some remark Churchill had made. She stood up shaking her fist and said "Mr Churchill you're an absolute disgrace, if you were married to me I'd poison your coffee!" Winston Churchill slowly rose to his feet and said "Lady Astor, if I was your husband, I'd drink it". Oh that Churchill. He had more one-liners than Del Boy. There's a statue of him on your right. The old bulldog.

Anyway, where was I? Speeches, wedding, tongues, blood, oh yeah, Duncan, that's right. We were in this hotel having a slow dance at the reception. I think the DJ was playing *Lady in Red* you know by Chris de Burgh. I love that song. And I was the lady in red. I was wearing my satin red dress and cream shoes from Christian Lacroix. I knew I looked good. In fact let's not mince words here, I looked *stunning.* I was the knees of ze bee. Anyway, Duncan held me close and whispered in my ear. He said:

AS DUNCAN: (Manchester accent.) Sand, how about you and me doing it?

And I said:

AS HERSELF: What? Here? In front of all these people?

And he said:

AS DUNCAN: No, get hitched. Tie the knot.

It was very romantic. He was a bit pissed of course. He'd had quite a bit to drink to get up confidence to make his Best Man speech. But I could tell he meant it. That he loved me. And of course I loved him. So I said *YES*!!! It was the happiest moment of my life up until then. I felt brilliant inside… then the music changed. I think it was Frankie Goes to Hollywood and *Two Tribes.* And he started dancing like men do when they're pissed. *(She imitates Duncan wildly dancing.)* And he fell over. Landed on Nikki-with-2Ks left thigh. The one with the blue garter on it.

We're now on Westminster Bridge crossing the river Thames. That's the real reason why London is here. Almost two thousand years ago the Romans came to the banks of the river Thames after they invaded this country in AD 43. They didn't know where the hell they were going, a bit like you lot really, but where they built a bridge over the river, they called the surrounding city Londinium. And this became London. Londinium isn't a Latin word in itself so we're not really sure where it came from. Of course I've got my own little theory about the name. Do you want to hear it? Yeah? All right then. Well I reckon there were probably already some people living here when the Romans arrived. Peasants I expect, just sitting around with their chickens and sheep and going about doing peasanty things. And the leader of the Romans probably went up to one of them and said 'What's this place called mate?' And the peasant probably grunted back '*Londinium*'. Which was probably an old British word meaning '*Sod off you bastards!*'

Anyway, where was I? Weddings, garters, proposals, Frankie Goes to Hollywood, oh yeah, Duncan. He asked me to marry him. My dad had a fit. My mum was all right, I think she fancied him herself. She always had a thing about a certain Australian actor.

AS HER MUM: (Warm London accent.) He's very sexy love. Sounds like a northern Johnny Depp but looks like Mel Gibson in *What Woman Want.*

But my dad …well he never liked Duncan. When I first took him home dad hardly said a word to him. He said he didn't like his manner.

AS HER DAD: (Strong Scottish accent.) I don't like him Sandra. Sounds like Johnny Vegas but looks like Mel Gibson in *Mad* bloody *Max*!

Which was a strange reaction considering Mel's

brilliant portrayal of William Wallace in *Braveheart*. But this woman wanted Duncan, so dad got overruled.

We got married in a registry office and it was the happiest day of my life. It was like walking down the aisle with you-know-who. Although there wasn't actually an aisle, it was more of a corridor – they had the builders in the main room – some kafuffle with the ceiling. I wanted to get married in a church, you know the full white wedding, but Duncan insisted on a registry office. Said he wasn't religious. So we got married in a civil ceremony in Cricklewood. It was all right though. But his mother… Oh don't talk to me about his mother. Don't start me off on her… Silly cow. Face like a raw turnip. We've never got on. Oh no. She never saw me as a good match for her precious Duncan. Never thought I'd make a good wife.

AS DUNCAN'S MUM: (Strong Chinese accent.)
You not good for him Sandcastle…
AS HERSELF: SANDIE!
AS DUNCAN'S MUM: You not good for him.

He special boy. You go away, leave him alone.
OK with you?

(With a smug grin.) If I knew then what I know
now…

St Thomas' Hospital on the right. A special place
for me 'cos it's where I was born. Honest. My
mum had come up to town to see Engelbert
Humperdinck at the Royal Albert Hall and went
into labour in the back row of the stalls.
Apparently her waters broke during the second
verse of *Please Release Me.* The ambulance got
here just in time. There's a museum here dedicated
to our greatest nurse Florence Nightingale, the
Lady with the Lamp. As opposed to me mum
who was the lady with the lump.

Just behind St Thomas' is Lambeth Palace, the
official London home to the Archbishop of
Canterbury. And beside that is St Mary at
Lambeth Church. That's where Captain Bligh of
Mutiny on the Bounty fame is buried. I love those
Bounty films don't you? Which one's your
favourite? Clark Gable? Marlon Brando? Mine's

the one with Mel Gibson in it. Whenever I see it I imagine my Duncan strutting about on the poop deck polishing his telescope. *(As Captain Bligh.)* Mr Christian, this is mutiny!

Now on the left is the old GLC building. The Greater London Council as was. Now it's all hotels and luxury apartments. In the bottom of it is the London Aquarium. Which is great if you're into fish. Duncan would often drag me in there. He's potty about tropical fish. Has all sorts. Rare ones too. Red Fire-fish, Blue-spotted-longfins, Spiny puffers. I don't know, they were all in our flat swimming about in this huge tank behind the telly. I used to think it was quite sophisticated really, like something out of *Dr No*. Fish are Duncan's biggest love. He buys them from this bloke in Milton Keynes who imports the rarest species from abroad. We would often drive down there on his Triumph and on the way back I would sit pillion behind him clutching these plastic bags of water containing these fish. Once, one of the bags burst and a Madeira Rockfish got stranded in the middle lane of the M25. My God! Duncan went mental. We stood helpless on the hard shoulder and watched as an *Ikea* van squashed the bugger flat. Still those fish used to make him happy. And if he was happy, I was happy. So there we all were. Him, me and the fish.

(*Pointing up to her right.*) Now do have a look at that ladies and gentlemen. The *London Eye*, the tallest observation wheel in the world. 135 metres high. Impressive isn't it? You step into one of those glass pods and up you go. Brilliant views. Have you heard about the latest craze to get married on it? It's true. Apparently you have to get married when you're right at the top. The highest point. Nothing else will do. You only have a few minutes to exchange your vows. Then like most marriages, it's downhill all the way…

She removes her blazer and puts it down on one of the front seats.

That's better. It's very sticky today isn't it? Mind you, we had good weather for our honeymoon, Duncan and I. Only rained one day in two weeks. We went to the Canaries. Tenerife. Duncan took lots of photos which he later developed himself in his shop. Just as well as some of them were a bit, well, racy. If they'd gone through Boots we'd probably have been arrested. It was really nice though. Just the three of us. Oh I didn't tell you did I? His mother came too. Cow. Didn't have any choice really. She paid for the trip. Got it at discount on account of her working part-time in a travel agent.

AS DUNCAN'S MUM: I give you nice present in Canary place, Sandbag...
AS HERSELF: SANDIE!
AS DUNCAN'S MUM: I give you nice present but cheaper deal for three than two. So I come too. OK with you?

She shakes her head at her mother-in-law's insensitivity then suddenly spots someone in the street.

Oh look! There's that actor what's-his-name. You know the one on the telly in that soap. You know who I mean. The one with the pudding basin haircut who's always being told about his bad breath. Thingy. What's-his-name? (*She waves.*)

Cooeee! Hello. *(She abruptly stops.) My God he gave me the finger!!* Maybe it's not him. Looks like him though. Dead ringer. You never know who you might spot as you go round London. You want to keep your eyes open. I once saw a breakfast television weather girl. I did. Can't remember her name now but she was the one who stood in front of the map with her huge boobs. Her left tit always blocked out Cornwall.

So when we got back from our honeymoon Duncan and me moved into his little flat in Cricklewood. It's above his shop actually. He did some sort of deal with the landlord. It was all right except for the smell of developer. God that gets up my nose. Terrible pong. Anyway, the flat is a bit small but we liked it. And of course Duncan didn't have far to go to work. Just down the stairs really so he could have a bit of a lie-in every morning, and more often than not a bit of the old morning glory…

AS DUNCAN: Not getting up just yet are you Sand?

Ah, we're now crossing Waterloo Bridge. The longest bridge in central London. This bridge is where we can see the two cities that make up London. On the left is the City of Westminster, nearly a thousand years old and on the right is the City of London almost two thousand years old and originally built by the Romans. It's amazin' innit? Sid, slow down so they can take some photos...

She takes a gulp from a plastic water bottle.

Anyway, after the wedding we moved into the little flat above *Well Developed.* I'd keep it nice and clean. You'd never have found any dust in there. Spotless. I was really happy. I didn't miss going out to clubs and stuff. I mean, after we'd finished at *Madame Bridget's,* me and the girls would often go out clubbing. Have a bit of a laugh. But what's it all about? You spend your life going out to meet men don't you? It's a game. Single women going out trying to meet single men and vice-versa. Trying to find Mr Right. Or *Mr Right Now!!* It's always been like that. And when you find what you think is the ideal bloke, you fall in love and marry him, if you're lucky. And then you settle down. And that's what we did. In Cricklewood above *Well Developed*.

On your right is Somerset House better known as the former offices of the General Register of Births, Deaths and Marriages. The hatch 'em, match 'em and dispatch 'em place. Anyway, we were really happy in our little flat. Apart from one thing. It was about this time that we discovered we couldn't have kids… You can imagine the pressure from his mother.

AS DUNCAN'S MUM: Why no kids, Sandpaper? My boy make good father. Get on with it. OK with you?

AS HERSELF: No it's not OK with me. Or him. Mind your own business, turnip face!

We're now approaching Covent Garden. There used to be a fruit, veg and flower market here once. Have you seen *My Fair Lady*? This was where Professor Henry Higgins first met Eliza Doolittle. I used to love that film when I was small. I would pretend I was Audrey Hepburn and my little brother Timmy would be Rex Harrison. I nearly choked once. Timmy kept trying to make me talk proper by filling me mouth with gobstoppers. Silly really. Timmy didn't look anything like Rex Harrison. He'd stand there in his short-trousers making me say 'The rain in Spain stays mainly in the plain' again and again. But I loved Rex Harrison. He was one of my first crushes. He was, honest. Him and that odd looking bloke in *Boney M. (She considers this.)* God, no wonder I turned out like I did.

The thing was Duncan and I really wanted kids. We really did. So we went for it hammer and tongs so to speak but nothing happened. I said we should both go and have tests and see what could be done. Duncan didn't want to do that though. I think he thought it was unmanly or something, going into a cubicle with a copy of *Razzle* and a jam-jar. So I secretly went and had my own tests and eventually discovered it was me who couldn't. God that came as a shock I can tell you. Some blockage somewhere. I never told Duncan, I just kept it to myself. I wish I had done now. I still did a bit of this, the tour guiding, in the summer anyway. Looking back it was probably the worst decision I made. You see during the summer people tend to take loads more pictures so Duncan was working twelve, fourteen hours a day developing and printing. It was all getting a bit much so he decided to do something. One day he said to me:

AS DUNCAN: I'm taking on an assistant, Sand.

And that's when *she* came into our life.

On the left is the London School of Economics. That's where Mick Jagger was a student but he left early 'cos he couldn't get no satisfaction.

Anyway, where was I? Oh yeah. Sonya Grey. She wasn't even very pretty. Long black hair and pinched features. I called her the *Hawk*. She had that sort of look as if she was about to swoop down from a height and claw a sheep. But that aside she seemed OK. She just came in at nine-thirty in the morning and stood behind the counter all day taking in people's rolls of film and working the till. Apparently she'd done something similar working in Wednesbury.

AS THE HAWK: (Flat, vacant Black Country accent.) If you want an extra set of prints we have a special 2 for 1 offer on. Quite a saving, I think you'll find.

Duncan was out the back in the dark room doing the real work. At least that's what I thought. But there's other things you can get up to in the dark of a dark room. Things started developing, if you know what I mean, between Duncan and the *Hawk* and I'm not talking Kodak paper here. I came back from work early one afternoon and could hear him and her in there. Heavy breathing and stuff. But you know it's very difficult if two people are at it in a dark room. You know they're in there but they have the perfect excuse for not unlocking the door.

AS DUNCAN: Just a few minutes love, there's a film developing. Be out in a moment.

It's hopeless. By the time you get in there it's all a

red glow and everybody's peering at strips of
negatives.

The *Hawk* tended to avoid the darkroom after
that but I knew something was going on. You just
know don't you?

(*Points to her left.*) Now here's a lovely little church.
St Clement Danes, the central church of the Royal
Air Force. The bell rings out the nursery rhyme
"*Oranges and Lemons*". Do you know that one? I
do. My nan used to sing it to me when I was small.
It's like a conversation between all the bells of all
the London churches. Do you want to hear a bit of
it? All right then. I'll see if I can remember it…

(*She sings.*)   "Oranges and lemons,
          Say the bells of St Clement's.
          Pancake and fritters,
          Say the bells of St Peter's.
          Two sticks and an apple,
          Say the bells at Whitechapel.
          You owe me five farthings,
          Say the bells at St Martin's.
          When will you pay me?

Say the bells at Old Bailey.
When I grow rich,
Say the bells at Shoreditch.
Pray, when will that be?
Say the bells at Stepney.
I'm sure I don't know,
Says the great bell at Bow.
Here comes a candle to light you to bed,
Here comes a chopper to chop off your head."

A beat. She immediately turns to her right.

Royal Courts of Justice on the left. The second highest civil court in the land. Civil litigation only. Suing someone or getting a divorce.

She pauses, reflecting on what she's said.

Anyway, so what was I to do? I was convinced Duncan was having an affair with the *Hawk* so I decided to turn detective. I reckon he'd got wind that I suspected something. Him and the *Hawk* didn't go in the dark room so much. In fact some days she didn't go in there at all. So where were they liasing? Because liasing they were. I was

40

convinced of that. He was meeting her somewhere. Most evenings he was out till quite late saying he was meeting business acquaintances. But I knew he was seeing her. I mean there's only so many *Well Developed* franchise holders around. He said I could always get hold of him in an emergency by texting him. Frustrating things texts aren't they? Occasionally I would leave a message like "Where R U and wot R U doing?" Talk about being naïve. As if he'd text me back and say "Shagging. Nearly finished. B home soon. Duncan." But I knew where he was anyway. You didn't have to be Inspector Morse to work that one out. There was only one place he could be. Round hers.

She turns and looks ahead.

That's Monument to Temple Bar and it's very significant. As soon as we pass it we enter the City of London. It's not very large, the City. About one square mile big.

So I decided to stake out the *Hawk's* place in Kilburn. Wasn't very grand. She lived in this grotty one bedroomed ground floor flat. It did have a little garden out the back though. All overgrown of course. Anyway, there was a tree about halfway down, perfect cover. I climbed over the wall at the back and set up position and on the very first night I saw them…

We hear a street newspaper vendor shouting 'Standard! Standard! Get it here.'

Oh, hold the front page! We're going down Fleet Street. For over 300 years this is where we published our newspapers. Not many papers here today though, they've all moved out. But some great writers started along this street. Arthur Conan Doyle, Charles Dickens, Jackie Collins. They all wrote for newspapers and magazines. Still there's one legacy left over from the journalistic days. The pubs! Fleet Street's a great place for a pub-crawl. There are more pubs along this street than almost anywhere else in London. Now there's a sobering thought…

So where was I? Grotty flat in Kilburn, stakeout, oh yeah, Duncan. I was watching the two of them in her kitchen. She was struggling to get the cork out of a bottle of wine. She just couldn't get it out so she passed it to Duncan. He was pulling and pulling with the bottle stuck between his legs. His face was getting redder and redder. And then it happened. His back went. He's always had a bad back. The slightest thing sets it off. You should see him, doubled-up like a Himalayan Sherpa. Well there was a real drama then. She was running around trying to help him and he kept saying…

AS DUNCAN: Don't touch me, don't touch me.
AS THE HAWK: What's the matter Dunky?
AS DUNCAN: Me back's gone…
AS THE HAWK: Lie on the bed, I'll rub it.
AS DUNCAN: NO!

It was a right fandango. I thought there's no point in me staying so I went home and knocked back half a bottle of vodka. I tried to imagine what I was going to say when Duncan came in. Shouldn't have bothered really. By the time he got back, all doubled up, from the *Hawk* I'd passed out on the sofa. I woke up in the morning with this cracking headache and there he was lying beside me on the floor fixing his back. He has to remain rigid for a minimum of three hours on the parquet. I didn't say anything that morning. About him and the *Hawk*. I hadn't actually seen anything. Not really. No, I had to get hard evidence.

Well it didn't take me long. Two weeks later I was busy doing me ironing when Duncan comes up from the shop and says he wants to talk to me. Something important he says.

AS DUNCAN: Could I have a word, Sand?
AS HERSELF: Of course Dunc.

Well, he only went and told me straight out he'd been sleeping with the *Hawk*. No hesitancy, no nothing.

AS DUNCAN: I think you should know that I've been seeing Sonya. We've been having a relationship.

AS HERSELF: Oh…

That really knocked me sideways. I mean I know

I already knew but for him just to tell me matter of factly like that, well, it cut through me like a knife. It really hurt inside. But nothing he said could prepare me for what was coming up. He then told me she was pregnant and was going to have his baby. By this time I didn't know where to look, my eyes were all over the place. I was looking in every direction but his. It was the bombshell from hell. I was speechless. Well as speechless as you can be when you're throwing an iron at someone. Mind you I didn't hit him. I don't know whether it was me eyes not looking at him or what but the bloody iron ended up in his flamin' aquarium! The top was off because earlier I'd been feeding them. There was this huge flash and all the fish got electrocuted. They were all floating on top of the water. He went berserk! Never mind him and the *Hawk*. He just went into one saying I'd deliberately murdered his precious Blue spotted-friggin'-longfin-wotsits!

AS DUNCAN: You bloody woman!! I'll never build a collection like that again!

He went mental! Well by this time I'd turned on the

waterworks. I was bawling and all that and he seemed to calm down a bit. So we tried to have a frank discussion about him and the *Hawk*. Didn't resolve anything. She was three months gone, he claimed he was in love with her and that night he moved out. As simple as that. Packed a suitcase and walked out. I felt so alone that night. Just me in that bloody flat. Me and a tankful of fish all floating on the surface and staring at me with dead eyes.

She turns and looks ahead.

There's St Paul's Cathedral. Wren's masterpiece. We'll be up there in a minute. Tell you more then.

Anyway, it always amazes me how quickly one recovers from something if you've got a goal. And I had a goal all right. I wanted Duncan back whether the *Hawk* was pregnant or not. I've been dumped too many times to realise that if you don't get in there straight away you lose ground. Strike while the iron's hot. And I had my opportunity because Duncan was still opening up the shop every day although he was actually living with her. By this time of course the *Hawk* wasn't working with him. I'd have throttled her if she'd taken one step over the threshold and she knew that. So I made it my business to go down and see him, bring him a cup of tea occasionally and that sort of thing. I think I threw him to be honest with you. Hell hath no fury and all that and there was I dropping down to see him every ten minutes like Mary flippin' Poppins.

The Old Bailey's on the left. Our Central Criminal Court. See the statue of Justice on top of the dome? I wonder what it's like to stand in the dock in there? At least they don't hang people anymore. Ruth Ellis was the last woman to be hanged in this country. July 13th 1955. She murdered someone for love. It's not as uncommon as you might think …

So there I was declaring my undying loyalty to the rat and to be honest I did still love him. I really did. Even after all he'd done I was still in love with him. And then there was an extraordinary turn of events…

Fade-up a peel of church bells.

St Paul's Cathedral. Took Christopher Wren thirty-five years to build and was opened in 1710 in the reign of Queen Anne. Of course we all remember St Paul's from 1981 don't we? This was where Prince Charles married Diana.

Fade-out the bells.

So where was I? Oh yeah, it was a Wednesday and I went down to see Duncan, took him a cup of tea. He was busy in the dark room but he said he wouldn't mind if I joined him. In fact he said he'd like the company. It was weird being in there in the dark with him. Just the red glow. Almost romantic in a funny sort of way. As he developed pictures of other people's holidays we started talking about this and that and to be honest we were getting on better than we had in months. He didn't mention the *Hawk*. I don't know whether it was deliberate or not. In fact I had to bring her into the conversation. I said something subtle like…

AS HERSELF: How are you getting on with wots-her-face?

And to my astonishment he said they'd been having filthy great rows, he'd been banned from the bedroom and was having to sleep in her front room.

AS DUNCAN: She's got me kipping on the sofa, Sand. With my back!

Well you could've knocked me down with a throwaway camera. I said what was the problem and he told me that he reckoned she had faked the pregnancy because now she claimed she had miscarried it and he didn't believe her. Well... I couldn't believe what I was hearing. It sounded too good to be true, if you know what I mean. The *Hawk* and him hardly talking and she not expecting any more. Talk about a turnaround. Anyway, you can guess what happened can't you? Yeah, that's right. It just felt right. Him and me thrashing about on the floor underneath the enlarger and fixing tanks. It was fantastic. Until afterwards. He got a text. From her. Don't ask me what it said but it must've been something lovey-dovey because the next thing he's pulling on his jeans and getting ready to go.

I said:

AS HERSELF: Where are you going then?

And he said:

AS DUNCAN: Back to hers.

So I said:

AS HERSELF: But I thought you were having terrible rows and kipping on the sofa hurting your back and all that.

And he said:

AS DUNCAN: I'm sorry, I can't help myself. I love her and I want to be with her.

And off he went. Just like that. The bastard. I felt used, cheated, crippled inside… It was at that precise moment that I knew I was going to have to cause him some serious grief. My head was exploding with it all…

BRING OUT YOUR DEAD! BRING OUT YOUR DEAD! That's what they were shouting in these very streets in the long, hot summer of 1665. The year of the Great Plague. The bubonic plague. The flea living on the rat spread it. They reckon about one hundred thousand died in all. A third of the population of London. It was appalling. Men walked up and down these streets shouting out 'Bring out your dead' so they could cart the corpses off to the plague pits. There was a terrible stench of rotting flesh 'cos they couldn't get 'em out fast enough. Mothers taught their children to sing a little rhyme as they played on the streets hoping it would ward off the fever. Some of you probably know it.

(She sings.)   'Ring, a ring o'roses
                A pocketful of posies.
                A-tishoo! A-tishoo!
                We all fall down.'

Anyone heard that? Let me tell you what it meant. 'Ring, a ring o'roses' was when you knew you'd caught the plague. You had a thumping hot temperature and a rash of rosy, red rings all over your body. 'A pocketful of posies' were the herbs and spices you'd have about your person to ward off the fever. Remember there was no medicine in those days. No antibiotics, nothing. 'A-tishoo! A-tishoo!' was when you started sneezing. Continuous sneezing was the final symptom. Once you started sneezing you knew you were going to die. 'We all fall down.' Well that was when you snuffed it. A terrible way to go.

On the left is St Mary-le-Bow church. Famous for its Bow Bells. They say that if you're born within the sound of Bow Bells you can call yourself a London Cockney.

Anyway where was I? Diseases, plague, rats. Oh yeah, Duncan. How was I going to get my own back? Punish him. Because that's what I had to do and let me tell you it's not that straightforward. Oh no. My first idea was to kill him. I know, I know, you probably think I'm completely mad. Alfreda Hitchcock. Well I probably was. I was so wound up inside. I didn't even think of any consequences. Duncan had hurt me beyond repair so the obvious solution was to get rid of him, permanently, so he could never, ever do it again. So, accept, that was my state of mind. Not normal I know but I'm sure all of you at some time have harboured similar thoughts. Anyway it was a pointless exercise. Even if you do want to kill your old man where do you find someone to do it? I mean you hardly flick through *Yellow Pages* looking under Contract Killers do you?

She mimes making a phone call.

AS HERSELF: Hello? Is that Contract Killers-r-us?
AS LONDON THUG: That's right. Want someone taken out?
AS HERSELF: Well I'm not sure. How do you actually do it?
AS LONDON THUG: You leave that with us little lady. We're the experts.
AS HERSELF: How much does it cost?
AS LONDON THUG: 25 grand.
AS HERSELF: Oh. Do you take Visa?

Oh hang about, I nearly forgot. The Great Fire. London had just got over the plague when the following September there was another disaster. The Great Fire of 1666. Started in Thomas Farriner's baker's shop over there in Pudding Lane. (*Points to her right.*) One night one of his ovens caught fire and to his horror it set alight the roof made of thatch. That ignited the building beside it, which in turn burnt down the next building and so on. Within four days and five nights four-fifths of London had burnt down. But, you know, sometimes two wrongs do make a right. 'Cos the fire wiped out the plague. Some say it destroyed the rats.

We're now on London Bridge.

(*She sings.*) 'London Bridge is falling down,
            Falling down, falling down.
            London Bridge is falling down.
            My fair lady'.

Oh, this is where they used to put the heads of executed prisoners. (*Pointing above her head.*) They'd stick 'em on the end of a pikestaff at the entrance to the bridge as a sort of warning to others. Hang on, I've got one of me *visual aids* somewhere. (*She dives into her bag and pulls out a transparent polythene bag containing the head of a man with long hair, blue facial war-paint and a ferocious stare. It is incredibly lifelike.*) The first ever head put up was William Wallace the Scottish patriot. Remember the movie *Braveheart*? Wooh!! He looks a bit angry doesn't he? (*She holds the head up to eye-level and stares at it.*) Hmm... reminds me of someone...

She puts the head down on a seat.

Anyway, I couldn't get someone to kill Duncan but I had to get at him somehow...

Oh by the way, just down here beside London Bridge is where the 'Nancy Steps' were. As in Charles Dickens's novel *Oliver Twist*. This is where Nancy betrayed Bill Sikes and he murdered her. Do you remember that? I do.

She stares down over the side of the bus for a beat and then continues.

It was over the next few weeks that things started

becoming clearer in my mind. I thought I'd try another angle. Don't do anything at all. Lay off Duncan. Give him a bit of space. I figured it wouldn't take too long for him to get bored with the *Hawk* and then he'd come back to me. And I'd forgive him and we'd start again and put all this dreadful business behind us. We might even adopt a baby. I liked that idea. I did. That we could be a little family and all that. In fact it gave me a certain piece of mind. It kept me going through that dark period when everything was topsy-turvy. My doctor put me on tranks which helped of course. To a certain extent anyway though now I'm not so sure that those pills didn't affect my mental judgement a bit. So there I was sort of floating along in limbo land waiting for Duncan to get bored with the *Hawk* when one day something awful happened. Have you ever had one of those days? When you think it just can't get any worse and then it does. That's what happened to me. I remember it so well. I'd been down Tesco's and had just stumbled back with me groceries when I saw a letter on the hall floor. It was from some solicitors informing me that Duncan was seeking a divorce. On some grounds or other. I couldn't take it in to be honest; I was that much shaking with anger. I immediately went downstairs to the shop to have it out with Duncan.

AS HERSELF: (Waving an imaginary letter.)
What's the meaning of this?

AS DUNCAN: I'm sorry if I've hurt you Sand but the fact is I'm in love with Sonya and I want to marry her. That's all there is to it.

Well, I lost it I'm afraid. I went mad. Swore at him and called him every name under the sun. I was appalling. Everything came out. Dark-rooms, fish tanks, Chinese mothers, you name it. Anyway there was no changing his mind. He wanted me out of the flat and out of his life. ASAP.

I just couldn't accept it. I didn't know what to do next. I knew I had to do something but what? This time I really did feel like killing him but that would've been too easy. Now I wanted revenge. I wanted Duncan to suffer for all the hell he had put me through. But killing him wasn't the answer. If I really wanted to cause him grief I had to hurt him in the strongest way possible. Make him really suffer. And in order to do that I'd have to kill *her*! The *Hawk*. And if I could do that … Well it just felt the right thing to do. And although I know I would never have been capable of killing Duncan, however much I now hated him, I was confident I was capable of killing *that cow.*

I think it was on a Thursday afternoon when I realised that the perfect time to kill the *Hawk* would be the following Saturday. Why? Because that particular Saturday was Duncan's birthday. What better day to kill her than on his birthday? That way he would be constantly reminded of her every year. Now all I had to do was come up with a foolproof method of murdering her.

I spent the next few weeks deep in research. I read anything that would provide me with a method of killing. I went to the library and took out Agatha Christies, Ruth Rendells, even old Sherlock Holmes stories. I did. But nothing was as inspirational as this place. (*Points to her left.*) The London Dungeon. London's horror museum. It shows you all the terrible things that have happened to London over the centuries. The fire, the plague, the rats, the torture, the blood, the gore, the horror, the fear, the terror… You name it; it's in there. It's like Madame Tussaud's Chamber of Horrors times ten!! It was mind provoking. Especially the Jack the Ripper stuff. You see, like him, I was after the perfect murder. One that could be suitably carried out without the slightest lead coming back to me. In a few weeks I became an authority on murder. I learnt how to poison, I learnt how to cause accidental death, I learnt how to kill in every manner possible. And not get caught. It's amazing you know. If you want to become a killer, there are more books to tell you how to do it than if you wanted to save life and train as a doctor. I became an authority on death. But strangely enough it was none of the methods I read about that became my final choice although I'm not saying that they didn't spark me off. My choice of the way I was going to kill the *Hawk* was all mine. It was totally my invention. And it was foolproof. It had to be. It had to be the perfect murder. One that even Columbo wouldn't be able to solve…

Distant heavy thunderclouds can be heard. From now to the end of the play it gets gradually more overcast.

Oh dear, rain's on its way. What a shame. Anyway, this was my plan, right? I'd get up as normal on the day, do a bit of housework, usual stuff. I'd then pop downstairs to the shop and say hello to Duncan.

AS HERSELF: Hello Duncan.
AS DUNCAN: Oh…er hi.

No doubt he'd be too busy to talk which would be fine by me. I'd probably wish him happy birthday though. I'd then ask him if I could borrow his little van to do some shopping. He'd be bound to say yes just to get me out of there. I'd then drive to where the *Hawk* lived, slip on a wig, sunglasses and a bit of lippy, go up to her front door and press her buzzer. She'd be surprised to see me of course; after all we hadn't spoken for months. Chances are she wouldn't recognise me straight away so I'd explain the wig was a new look I was trying out. She'd probably make a few derogatory remarks saying it didn't suit me or something…

AS THE HAWK: Don't mean to be funny but that colour doesn't really suit you.

…as if she'd know anything about style, then before she could ask me why I'd called round I'd tell her that I'd come to terms with Duncan leaving me and setting up with her and now just needed to clear the air with her. She wouldn't want me in there, that's for sure, but I'd just push past her anyway and go straight into her lounge. Now I knew this next bit would upset me. I'd have to steel meself. Many of Duncan's things would be in that room. I've envisaged it so many times in my mind. His books. A framed photo of him and her on the mantelpiece perhaps. One of his jackets slung on the back of a chair the way he always used to do… It would all be so bloody cosy. But of course running alongside the wall would be his beloved aquarium. *THAT BLOODY FISH TANK MEANT EVERYTHING TO DUNCAN.* The day he came back for it and took it out of our flat was the day that I knew he wasn't coming back. Ever. But little did anyone know that glass receptacle was going to provide me with my method of killing her. To give the *Hawk* her due I'd imagine she'd try and accommodate my visit. She'd offer me a drink…

AS THE HAWK: Fancy a cuppa?

…and I'd say yes although I knew I wouldn't be drinking it. I wouldn't even touch the cup. No way. I wouldn't want anything to incriminate me. Nothing should show that I was ever in that flat.

So whilst she'd be dithering about in her kitchen, I'd slip on a pair of Marigolds that I'd have in my bag, nip over to the aquarium and open the top. I can imagine all the little fish immediately coming up to the surface with their little mouths opening and closing. Chances are she'd have forgotten to feed them…

AS THE HAWK: I'm always forgetting to feed his fish.

I'd then take a plastic bag out and rip it open. A

torrent of water would flood out into the tank.
There'd be a vibrant flash of colour, velvety
orange-brown and blue stripes would slip under
the surface. I'd then look around for something to
drop in there. Could be anything. An ornament
off the mantelpiece, a paperweight, a flowerpot, it
doesn't matter. As long as it sunk to the bottom of
the tank. I'd then close the lid on the aquarium,
take my rubber gloves off and sit down.

Another clap of thunder.

The *Hawk* would then come in with her tray of
tea things and join me. She'd probably start
making small talk, chat away about something that
in her pea-sized brain was important…

AS THE HAWK: Did you see *EastEnders* last
night?

…and then I'd suddenly look over to the
aquarium with an innocent puzzled look and ask
her why the object was in there under the water?
The look on her face would be a picture.

AS THE HAWK: What's that doing in there? That shouldn't be in there.

She wouldn't be able to understand it at all. There'd be total bewilderment. Her one brain cell would be on time-and-a-half. She'd go over to the tank. I'd follow her. She'd open the top and plunge her hand into the water to get the object out. And then it'd happen... *She'd scream with the pain.*

A huge clap of thunder.

The tailfins of the Indian Ocean Clown surgeonfish exude a horrible poison. Just like I read in one of Duncan's fish books that he'd accidentally left behind in the flat. Very painful. So whilst she was running around in agony I'd pick up the nearest heavy object (maybe the teapot?) and bring it down on her head. Klunk!! She'd be out cold. Simple. The *Hawk* would be lying there on the carpet. But I wouldn't gloat. Oh no. Too much to do.

I'd wrap her up in some bin-liners, drag her

outside and dump her in the back of the van. Oh hold on a tick, here comes the Tower of London. I'll tell you the rest in a minute. Better put your brollys up as we cross Tower Bridge though. Here it comes...

Heavy rain starts to fall.

Ever since William the Conqueror built the original Tower with his brother around 1078, this castle has been associated with imprisonment, torture and execution. Seven people have had their heads cut off here including Anne Boleyn and Catherine Howard, two of King Henry VIII's six wives. They'd be led onto the executioner's block and PHEWWW!!! Off came their heads. In one cut of the axe if they were lucky. They were decapitated, beheaded, topped, whatever you like to call it...

More thunder.

So where was I? Oh yes, I've bungled the *Hawk* into the back of the van. Nobody sees me do it. I'd then drive down to an isolated part of the

Thames that I know, remove her clothes and throw her into the water. It'd be that easy. It really would. The body would go off with the current and that'd be the end of it. Until later of course. The police would be bound to find the body at some stage and fish it out. Duncan would have reported her missing and presumably he'd be asked to go and see if he could identify her. But of course he wouldn't be able to. Because just before I threw her in the river *I cut her head off!*

She quickly pulls out a transparent polythene bag containing a woman's head with long black hair. It is grotesque.

Oh no, this isn't her. This is Anne Boleyn. One of me *visual aids*. Ugly old cow, isn't she? I'll put her head back in my bag.

She puts the head back in the bag and zips it up.

A brilliant plan, wouldn't you agree ladies and gentlemen? Unfortunately I never found out whether it would have worked or not because something extraordinary happened…

When I arrived at her flat, all dolled up in my wig and what-have-you, the Hawk was coming out with loads of suitcases and piling them into the back of a taxi. Despite my careful disguise, she recognised me straight away…

AS THE HAWK: Oh hello, what are you doing here?

She told me that she'd found out that Duncan was having an affair with some trollop called Tina.

AS THE HAWK: He's shagging the cow. She owns the Dollis Hill franchise for *Well Developed.*

Well. Would you believe it? The *Hawk* apparently had had enough and was off to live with her sister in Sutton Coldfield. She'd known about the affair for a while but had decided to move out today as it was his birthday. I thought great minds think alike. She then said the landlord wanted the flat vacant ASAP so he could move in some Russian students. Would I mind asking

Duncan to pick up his fish tank?
Would I mind? I said I'd be delighted.

A pause.

Trouble is Duncan's disappeared. No one's seen or
heard of him for weeks. He's completely vanished.
God knows where he is. If you see him, tell him to
get in touch. You can't miss him; he's the spitting
image of Mel Gibson.

Well, that's the end of my tour folks. Welcome to
London…

*She unplugs her microphone and carrying her
holdall, starts to walk down the stairs. She
suddenly remembers something and re-appears.*

Silly old me, I forgot me head…

*She picks up the William Wallace/Mel Gibson
head from the seat and exits.*

Blackout.

Laugh? I Nearly Went To Miami!

A comedy by Miles Tredinnick

(1 set, 4 men, 3 women)

Laugh? I Nearly Went to Miami! is a zany and fast moving comedy of confusion. When Tom Weals, an Elvis fanatic, and Alice his fiancee are unable, due to fog, to fly to Miami for an Elvis Presley Convention, they arrive back at Tom's flat to find that they have inadvertently picked up the wrong suitcases at the airport and are now in possession of half a million dollars. Further confusion arises with the arrival of, firstly, Tom's flashy brother Barney, who is hoping to use the flat to seduce Muriel, his latest girlfriend and is none too pleased to find Tom at home, then Alice's eccentric Auntie with a bag containing $20,000 (a wedding present for Tom and Alice) then Frankie, a thug working for the owner of the suitcase dollars, whom Tom & Alice assume is a member of the local constabulary, and finally, Inspector Hendy, a real policeman, who somehow manages to sort everything out!

Laugh? I Nearly Went To Miami! is available from
Samuel French Ltd
(ISBN 057301633)

It's Now Or Never!

A comedy by Miles Tredinnick

(1 set, 4 men, 3 women)

It's Now or Never! is the sequel to the earlier stage comedy
Laugh? I Nearly Went to Miami!

Elvis Presley fanatic Tom Weals and his fiancee Alice arrive in
Spain from Colchester in preparation for their long-awaited
wedding. Keith Clark, a fellow Elvis fanatic, has offered them
the use of his villa outside Marbella whilst he is in London,
but their arrival has been predated by a sighting by Keith of
the real Elvis alive and hiding out in a nearby villa.
Unbeknownest to Alice, who is not much of an Elvis fan,
Keith talks Tom into helping him kidnap Elvis and sell the
story to the British tabloid press. Things go according to plan
until the victim appears to die in their custody. The ensuing
confusion resulting from the attempts to hide their
adventures (and the body) from Alice while convincing the
Sunday Insider of their conquest leads to chaos as a variety of
Elvises appear and disappear and identities change by the
moment in this fast-paced and frenetic comedy.

It's Now Or Never! is available from
Josef Weinberger Plays Ltd
(ISBN 0856761486)

Printed in the United Kingdom
by Lightning Source UK Ltd.
124965UK00001B/67-69/A